1

Small Animal Ornaments:

Sparrow, Fancy Sparrows, Hummingbird, Winged Bird

Snail and Tiny Butterfly, Sleeping Cat, Penguin and Owl

Copyright 2010

Susan D. Kennedy

These little crocheted animals and birds are my obsession: they are so incredibly fast to make and satisfying to hang, clip on to a barrette, or give away. They're smiles in crochet form! I hope you enjoy them as much as I do. I designed them to be based upon a small foundation chain or a circle of double crochets. They are quick as a

2

snap, but might be a bit difficult if you're not used to working with small patterns or my "long" single crochet stitch.

I'd recommend that you make the design first in a larger yarn with a standard hook, and then when you have perfected it, move on to smaller threads, if you wish. Sometimes working these thread crochet projects in yarn will bring about a little distortion in shape, but they will work out right when you shift back to fashion crochet thread or traditional crochet thread.

A note about my "long single crochet" stitch which is the final step in finishing some of these birds: While the basic shape of the bird is done in traditional chains, single crochet, double crochet and triple crochet stitches, the next round will be worked in an elongated single crochet stitch which covers the previous stitches entirely. I call these "long single crochet" stitches. (Lsc) You will insert your hook way down into those original chain stitches at the center of the bird, yarn over way up high at the back of the edge, and finish the single crochet. It will have a very long "post", actually it will consist of long threads which extend upwards from the center of the bird to the edge, where the rest of the stitch is looped and completed. These "long single crochet" stitches serve as decorative stitches which give the ornament a puffy, sleek look, with chain stitch shapes visible only at the edges. It's fun! Try it! Here is my video showing how I do it, for those of you who are e-book buyers:

http://picasaweb.google.com/susanlinnstudio/VideoLongSingleCrochet?authkey=Gv1sRgCPqYgJOW29GavQE#5524280800651846450

Abbreviations:

Ch   chain

Dc   double crochet

Dtc   double triple crochet (yarn over three times)

Hdc   half double crochet (yarn over as for a dc, but take off all three loops at once, forming a shorter stitch than a dc, and a fuller, slightly taller stitch than a sc.

Lsc   long single crochet
         (explained above)

Prev   previous

Rnd   round

Sc   single crochet

Sl St   slip stitch

St   stitch

Tc   triple crochet

Small Bird Ornament

(Sparrow)

Pattern "S"

This is my basic bird pattern, very tiny – perhaps an inch and a half or two inches when worked in thread crochet. You will find the variations in the next section of this booklet which make it fancier and give it wings, tails and legs. This simple basic bird can be used as a quick Christmas ornament or as an appliqué for sewing projects. It's happy and quick as a snap, but might be a bit difficult if you're not used to working with small patterns or my "long" single crochet stitch.

A helpful diagram for the basic sparrow pattern is included below which shows the very few stitches which comprise the base shape of the bird.

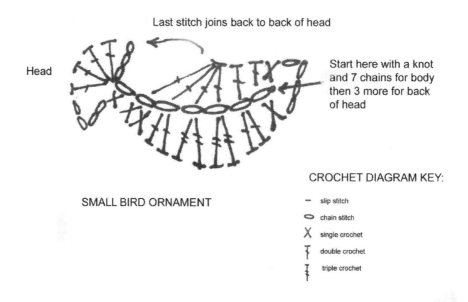

Last stitch joins back to back of head

Head

Start here with a knot and 7 chains for body then 3 more for back of head

CROCHET DIAGRAM KEY:

— slip stitch

⬭ chain stitch

X single crochet

Ŧ double crochet

Ŧ triple crochet

SMALL BIRD ORNAMENT

This little ornament and all of the others to follow are worked in crochet thread with a steel crochet hook (I used a size 4 when using just one thread, and I used a larger aluminum size F hook when I used a doubled up thread on the larger bird).

Working your basic bird ornament:

You are starting at the tail end of the bird. As you start, tighten the knot of your first ch so it will not loosen when you are working the tail of the bird. Do not count this knot as a ch. Ch 10, (These are your 7 **foundation chain** stitches plus 3 more that count as a first dc), then (4 dc, ch 4 –*this is the beak* – 1 sc) all in the 4th ch from the hook. Continuing in a counter-clockwise motion around the initial chains, work 2 sc in next ch, 2 dc in next ch, 2 tc in next 2 ch, 2 dc in next ch, sc in last chain. Ch 4 (this will be the tail), continue counter-clockwise up and around the tail: sc, dc in same (last) ch, dc in next ch, make decreasing dc in next 4 chains, holding the last loop of each dc on the hook, then yarning over and removing these last loops at the end (this is like a decreasing stitch, or similar to a cluster See my video on decreasing dc stitches like this:

http://picasaweb.google.com/114014580264000126010/VideoDecreasingDC?authk ey=Gv1sRgCJCjmc_q4ebp3QE#5524271352199569394). Join to back of bird's head to finish. Do not cut thread.

Covering bird in long single crochet stitch:

Insert your hook way down into the initial ch at the center of the bird's head (ch number 7) and make long single crochet stitches all the way around the head. See video about making these stitches:

http://picasaweb.google.com/susanlinnstudio/VideoLongSingleCrochet?authkey=Gv 1sRgCPqYgJOW29GavQE#5524280800651846450

As you are working these stitches around head, (Sc, ch 2, sc) in ch-sp which forms beak (you have turned around and followed the beak and are now under the bird's chin. Insert your hook in next base ch and make 2 lsc. Work 2 lsc in each chain of bird's base, adding more lsc stitches if it seems to be necessary to cover the earlier stitches. Make sc, ch 4, sc in tail ch-4 sp, work 2 lsc in next ch, then decreasing lsc's in final stitches. (This will be inserting your hook, yarning over, inserting your hook, yarning over, etc, four times, then taking all loops off your hook at the same time to make cluster of lsc's. join to back of bird's head and tie off.

An alternate to finishing your bird with lsc's is one you can see on the right front part of the photo on page 1: the bird on the right, instead of being finished completely with lsc's, had its wing area outlined in simple chain stitches worked across its back, embroidery-style.

Have fun with your birds!

Read on for Variations of this bird which transform it into a snazzy bird with legs, wings, and fancy tails!

Sparrow Ornament Variations:

Pattern "S1"

You can vary your basic small bird ornament (pattern "S") by working the decorative rnd 2 with sc's and chains mixed in with your long single crochet stitch:

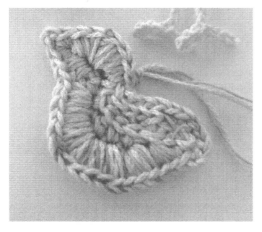

In this **winged bird**, Cover sparrow bird with long single crochet stitches as described above for rnd 2, but stop after the tail and continue along the edge of the back, counterclockwise, with a simple slip stitch which gives you a decorative chain shape along the edge. When you reach the back of the neck, double back and create the outline of a wing with chain stitches worked through the body of the work, curving to the tail and back toward the neck as shown in the photo.

In this **fancy bird** at right with a curly tail, there is a decorative element added with the doubled-up strand of thread that you can see. The dc's of the first round of the bird was worked with a strand of brown crochet thread as well as a strand of variegated pastel-colored crochet thread, used as one strand. It gives the bird a tweedy look, almost like the speckles you can see in the breast of a sparrow.

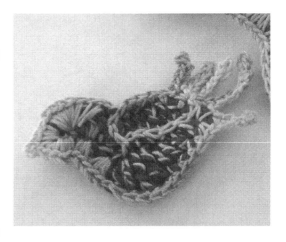

Also, when you get to round 2, you will start with long single crochet stitches as usual until you reach the throat, then work slip stitches along the belly to leave the pretty dc and tc stitches showing. As you approach the tail with your slip stitches, create your own versions of a curly tail: for example, ch 7, turn, then sc back on top

of the 7 chs to the back of the bird. Sl st in bird's body, then ch 9, turn, sc back on top of 9 chs as before, sl st to body, ch 7 and repeat scs to body, then ch 5, sc back to body, and ch 5, sc back to body. Vary the tail to express your own personality! These curls will need to be stiffened with a bit of fabric stiffener or white glue to make them curl the way you want to. After your tail feathers are done, continue to sl st counterclockwise along bird's back, then create a wing in chain stitches across the body of your work, as in the "winged bird" above.

In the colorful bird above, the edge stitches are the same, as well as working in a double strand of thread (one of which is a variegated pastel). Only the tail is

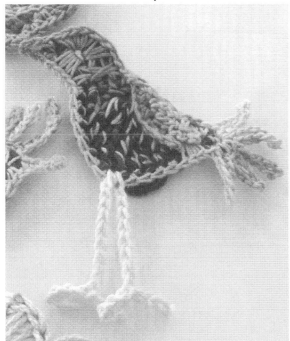

different, a group of ch, 2 dc, and ch which are worked in the ch-sp from rnd 1.

For this fanciful **tall bird** at left, Work as in the fancy bird above, but when you reach the back of the bird's neck, fashion a wing like this:

Wing: Ch 9 (making a chain away from the body), turn, skip 1 ch, 8 sc in next 8 ch, turn, sl st in 1st sc, ch 4, tc in 2nd sc, tc in 3rd sc, ch 5, join to 8th sc and tie off. You will need to stiffen this wing so that the tc's lay flat against the sc row.

Legs: Attach yellow crochet thread to desired place on bird's belly, leaving a long 2 foot length of thread on either side of the knot, one for each leg. With one of the lengths of thread, Ch 13, then sl st to join securely to 6th ch from hook (front of foot formed), then ch 3 and tie off for back part of foot. Repeat for second leg with the second length of thread. Tie off and weave ends through back of work.

Hummingbird Ornament or Appliqué

Pattern "H"

This little ornament, like the birds above, is mostly a single round of stitches of varying height, all worked counterclockwise on top of a length of foundation chains. As you form the bird's head, you will notice that the beak is nothing more than a floppy length of chain stitches: don't worry, when you pin this loop to a piece of cardboard and stiffen it with fabric stiffener or white glue, it will look like a hummer's beak! This little guy is a bit tricky, but when you get used to it, he's a snap to make. You can make the second round of decorative stitches in whatever colors you choose, making the wings and throat beautiful and unique. Have fun!

Before beginning this piece, tighten slip knot into knot to secure end of bird (so it doesn't ravel). *See diagram below which illustrates the first part of this ornament. A key to symbols can be found with the bird diagram on the fourth page of this document.*

Starting at arrow at far left of diagram, Ch 14. This is the **foundation chain.**

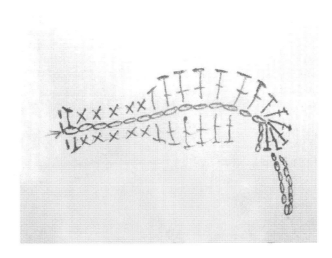

Rnd 1: ch 3 (counts as first dc), dc in 4th ch from hook, ch 12 (this will be the beak) join securely to top of dc just worked so end of beak is tight, work counterclockwise around top of head as follows: 5 dc in same ch, dc in next 6 foundation chs, hdc in next ch, sc in next 5 chs, hdc in last ch (you should be back at your beginning knot). Ch across to opposite side of tail, ch 2(counts as hdc on belly side of bird), sc in next 5 foundation chains opposite 5 sc on other side, hdc in next ch, dc in next 5 ch, join to 2nd ch of beginning ch-3 of rnd 1. You should have a wingless bird. Do not tie off, but continue below:

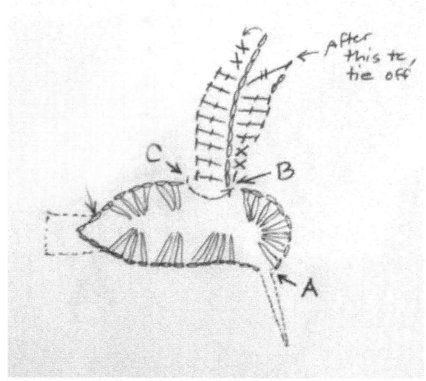

Rnd 2: covering the bird in long single crochets and forming the wings: *(see diagram above)*

Pass thread behind beak and at point A, begin lsc stitches discussed on page 1 and in this video:

http://picasaweb.google.com/susanlinnstudio/VideoLongSingleCrochet?authkey=Gv1sRgCP qYgJOW29GavQE#5524280800651846450

From point A, work lsc stitches, inserting hook at a point in the center of the bird's head. Work counterclockwise, and when you reach point B, start on main wing

(this is the wing on the left. After it is worked, you will sl st across to point B again and work the second wing on the right, then you will tie off.)

To make main wing,(the one on the left) ch 11, then rotate counterclockwise, and, skipping 1st ch on hook, work 2 sc then 8dc in next 10 ch stitches of wing. Sl st across , still working counterclockwise under the bird's wing back to point B and work second wing on top of first wing: sl st to first ch, work 2 sc, 4dc in next 6 stitches, then ch 2, tc in next stitch. This is the tip of the smaller wing. Tie off.

14

Finish the rest of rnd 2: Attach thread at point C and work lsc as in diagram down the bird's back. Insert your hook in various points, according to your judgment and design needs. When you reach bird's tail, ch stitch across base of bird to other side of tail, and continue around with lsc stitches, working counterclockwise toward the beak. Tie off when you reach beak.

You will need to stiffen the beak with fabric stiffener, or, in a pinch, white glue. (before this, it will be a floppy loop!). After dabbing a small amount on the beak, pin the beak and the back of the bird's head to a piece of cardboard and dab away excess stiffener.

Winged Bird (Bluebird) Ornament

Pattern "B"

This little crochet birdie is perfect for a tiny ornament for a Christmas tree, or as an appliqué for sewing projects. You can make variations shown below: a cardinal, a dove which is a bit different, and a crocheted bird "lariat" necklace. It's happy and quick as a snap, but might be a bit difficult if you're not used to working with small patterns or my "long" single crochet stitch.

I'd recommend that you make the design first in a larger yarn with a standard hook, then, when you have perfected it, move on to smaller threads, if you wish.

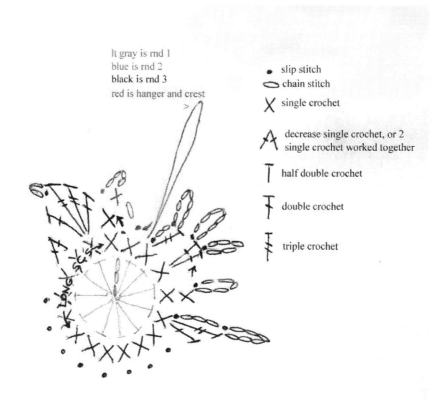

A helpful diagram is included above which shows the very few stitches which comprise the base shape of the bird.

Materials:

To make a bird approx. 2" across, I recommend using **crochet thread** (one single strand or two held together) and a **size 1 steel crochet hook**. Smaller hooks are an option, just experiment and find what feels best for you, but do bear in mind that changing thread gauge and hook size by very much can distort the design. But there are only a handful of stitches in the whole bird, so try lots of different approaches!

Working your bird ornament:

For this project, to make a bird approx. 2" across, I recommend using crochet thread (one single strand or two held together) and a size 1 steel crochet hook. Smaller hooks are an option, just experiment and find what feels best for you, but do bear in mind that changing thread gauge and hook size by very much can distort the design. But there are only a handful of stitches in the whole bird, so try lots of different approaches!

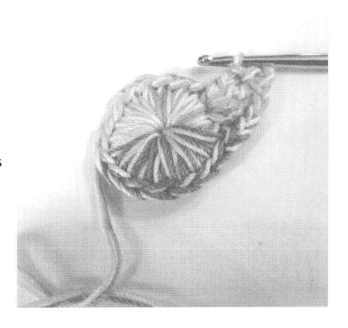

Ch 3, (slightly loose chains), join to form small ring.

Rnd 1: ch 3, 11 dc in ring.

Rnd 2: Cover the circular body you just finished with 18 lsc (*see this video on my "long single crochet" stitch, a single crochet in which you insert your hook all the way to the center of the disc so as to cover prev dc's completely around ring,* http://picasaweb.google.com/susanlinnstudio/VideoLongSingleCrochet?authkey=Gv 1sRgCPqYgJOW29GavQE#). Join.

Rnd 3: sc in first lsc, (dc, 2 tc) in next lsc, ch 2 (**beak made**), join to top of last tc worked, dc in same place, decr sc in next 2 lsc's –*in other words, sc two stitches together: insert hook, yarn over, pull thread through, insert hook in 2nd place, yarn over, pull thread through, then yarn over and pull all three loops off the hook together,* (**head made**), sl st in next 8 lsc's, (dc, tc in same lsc), ch 6, join to top of tc just worked, ch 3, join to same lsc, (**tail made, all in the same lsc**), sc in next lsc,

work ch 5, join to top of sc just worked, dc in next lsc, ch 5, join to top of dc just worked, dc in same lsc, ch 7, join to top of dc just worked, tc in next lsc, ch 7, join to top of tc just worked, ch 3, join to body of bird at same lsc as last tc. (**wing made**).

At this point, stop and pull a loop of your working thread through and knot it to form a hanger if you wish. (see photo above.) This is the stopping point for a bird with no crest/bluebird.

Other finishing options:

To add a crest for a cardinal or other bird, continue to work 1 sl st in next 2 lsc, ch 1, sc in same place, ch 4, join to next lsc and tie off.(**crest made**) For a smaller crest, you can work ch-3 instead of ch-4 in the last portion of the crest.

To add decorative lsc stitches to the head which gives a nice embroidery-like touch,

(you can see an example of this in the main photo of the multicolored bird on page 1), after finishing the bird as instructed above, don't tie off, but sl st once if needed to get into position at the back of the head, then work 5 lsc, inserting your hook all the way down to the bird's throat (see photo at left). Tie off and work end through stitches.

To make a dove variation with a longer and differently shaped tail and a larger wing, insert an extra tc before the tc in the tail instructions, then chain 1 more for a total of ch-7 for the tail. On the wing, add a chain to each of the feather-tip chains: for the first "feather" chain section, ch 6; on the next "feather" chain 6, on the next ch 7, and on the last, ch 8. You'll be surprised how different the bird will look, and if done in white, will make a beautiful tiny Christmas ornament to give away!

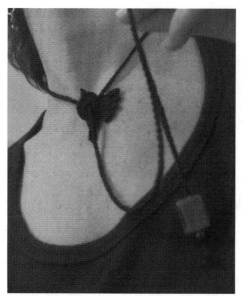

To make a bird "lariat", you can form your bird intentionally with a bit more of a hole in its center. To do this, begin your bird with a ch-4 (or for some types of thread, even a ch-5) instead of a ch-3. You can even substitute sc's for dc's in rnd 1 so as to alter the bird and make it more appropriate for a lariat. In the example at right, I began with a ch-4 ring and used sc in rnd 1 instead of dc. Then when I reached the end of the bird stitches, instead of tying off at the back of the bird's neck, I chained for approximately 22 inches (for me, this was 240 chains). Then I cut the end of the string, threaded it through the center hole of the bird, from back to front, and knotted the end of the chain (but left a few inches of thread for what follows); I then finished the end of the lariat with a few decorative beads.

This is a bird that will definitely need a little fabric stiffener and "blocking" (that is, stretching slightly and pinning to a board. Dab some full-strength fabric stiffener on the crest, wing, beak, and tail of your bird; place it on a plastic-covered piece of cardboard, press out any extra stiffener with a paper towel. (White glue can be substituted in a pinch). With straight pins, pull out the tips of the feathers and pin them, pull out the peak of the beak and pin it, etc, until the bird looks like you want it. (See photo below). Let dry for at least two hours.

Note: these instructions work well for crochet thread, fashion crochet thread, or a doubled up strand of crochet thread. If you plan to modify this pattern for a larger thread or yarn, you may find that you'll need to modify the number of stitches: if the beak looks too short, add a chain; if the tail seems to be starting too early, push it back a stitch or two. You'll be able to figure out how to adapt a small pattern for larger threads, it's really a matter for judgment regarding each particular thread.

Sid the Snail

Pattern "SN"

This little thread crochet snail is very quick, and fairly small; it uses a double triple (also called a double treble) crochet stitch. If you're not familiar with it, it's simply one more yarn over than a double crochet, treated in much the same way: simply take loops off by twos when finishing the stitch. Here is a helpful video of a double treble crochet: http://www.youtube.com/watch?v=-Ehv1Defp-U

I'd recommend that you make the design first in a larger yarn with a standard hook, and when you have perfected it, move on to smaller threads, if you wish. The pattern will be a bit distorted with larger yarns, but after one practice run, you'll be able to make the switch to thread crochet.

A helpful diagram is included below which shows the very few stitches which comprise the shape of the snail.

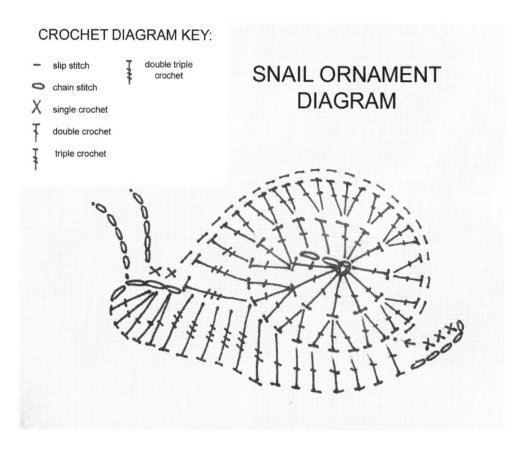

CROCHET DIAGRAM KEY:

- — slip stitch
- chain stitch
- X single crochet
- double crochet
- triple crochet
- double triple crochet

SNAIL ORNAMENT DIAGRAM

Materials:

To make a snail approx. 2" long, I recommend using **crochet thread** (one single strand or two held together) or fashion crochet thread (which is a bit puffier) and a **size 4 steel crochet hook,** Smaller hooks are an option for a nice tight teeny ornament; just experiment and find what feels best for you, but do bear in mind that changing thread gauge and hook size by very much can distort the design. There is an option in bold typeface for a baby snail, which varies only in that some stitches are left out or changed to sc instead of dc.

Working your Snail Ornament:

Ch 3, join to form small ring.

Rnd 1: Snail Shell:

Ch 2, 10 dc in ring.

(notice that you are approaching the original ch-2; you will not be joining, but will continue to work in a spiral to form a snail shell shape!);

Working only in back loop of all chains and stitches while working on shell,

dc in 1st chain of rnd 1, dc in 2nd chain of rnd 1, 3 dc in next 2 dc, *(2 dc in next dc, 3 dc in next dc), repeat from * for a total of 38 stitches **(23 for baby snail)**, including first 10 dc. *(You should have a noticeable spiral design outlined by the front loop of all of the dc's).*

Continue on to:

work 2 dc in next 4 dc, for a total of 46 dc. **(this will be 31 for baby)**

Work tc in next dc, then dtr in next 2 dc. (Shell made)

Rnd 2: Body: Change color, if desired (attach thread to back loop of the last dtc worked)

Ch 4, turn.

Rnd 3: Body, continued:

3 dc in 3rd ch from hook, 2 dc in next ch, tc in top of last dtc of shell, and, *rotating work to crochet along the side of the last dtc of the shell* , work 4 dtc **(4 tc for baby snail)** along the post of the same last dtc,

23

then dtc in the base of the same dtc

(right at the point where you are reaching the spiral shape of the shell),

then tc in back loop of next stitch, dc in back loops of next 7 dc's of shell, **(change these 7 dc's into 2 dc's and 5 sc's for the baby snail)** then for tail: ch 5.

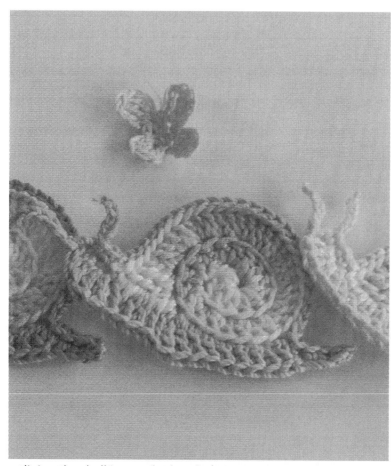

Rnd 4: Tail: working back toward shell, skip 1 ch, sc in next 3 chs just made, join to base of last dc worked *(where the body meets the shell).*

Rnd 5: Outlining the shell and forming tentacles:

Sl st in back loop of dc's of the shell, working counterclockwise from tail towards head. *(This will make a decorative line of stitches outlining the shell in your body color).*

When you reach the head, sc in first 2 stitches, then ch 5 for first tentacle. Cut thread, tighten and tie a knot; Reattach thread 1 stitch away for a ch-5 length for the second tentacle. Cut thread, tighten and tie knot again. Hide loose ends of your threads by weaving through work.

24

Starch snail if desired, or use a touch of fabric stiffener or white glue to shape its tentacles.

Tiny Butterfly Buddy of Sid:

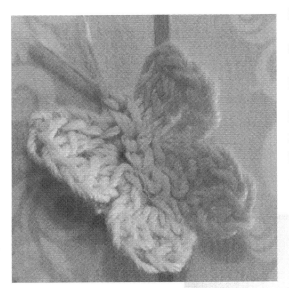

Instructions:

Ch 4, turn. This is your foundation chain.

Rnd 1: ch 1, Sc in 4 chains just worked, turn.

Rnd 2: ch 3, 2 dc in last sc from prev rnd. Ch 2, sl st in same sc, sl st in next 2 sc, ch 4, 2 tc in last sc, ch 3, join to same sc. Ch 1 and move across to other side of butterfly.

Rnd 3:

Sl st in 1st stitch of left side. These "stitches" are actually the other side of the beginning foundation chain.

Ch 4, 2 tc in same ch on body, ch 4, sl st in same ch, sl st in next 2 chains, (ch 3, 2dc, ch 2) in last sc, join at base of cluster. Sl st to base of butterfly's body and

After this point, slip stitch across to center of butterfly and chain stitch up center of back. Tie off.

Start here

TINY BUTTERFLY

chain stitch (for decoration) up the middle of butterfly's body, tie knot, and if possible, split thread into two antennae. You may stiffen these antennae with fabric stiffener and trim.

Diluted fabric stiffener (or, in a pinch, white glue) will also stiffen the butterfly's wings, if desired, and make them pose as you wish.

Enjoy your snail family and its butterfly friends!

Small Sleeping Cat Ornament

Pattern "C"

This little crochet cat is darling as a tiny ornament for a Christmas tree, or as an appliqué for sewing projects or hair accessories. It's a very small and quick thread crochet project, but might be a bit difficult if you're not used to working with small patterns or my "long" single crochet stitch.

I'd recommend that you make the design first in a larger yarn with a standard hook, and then when you have perfected it, move on to smaller threads, if you wish. The pattern will be a bit distorted with larger yarns, but after one or two prototypes, the tiny ones will be a snap!

A note about my "long single crochet" stitch which is an option that is given for working along the back, towards the tail: While the basic shape of the cat is done in dc and tc, the lsc (long single crochet) is an elongated single crochet stitch which covers the previous stitches entirely. You will insert your hook way down into the previous round of the piece, yarn over way up high at the back of the edge, and finish the single crochet. It will have a very long "post", actually it will consist of long

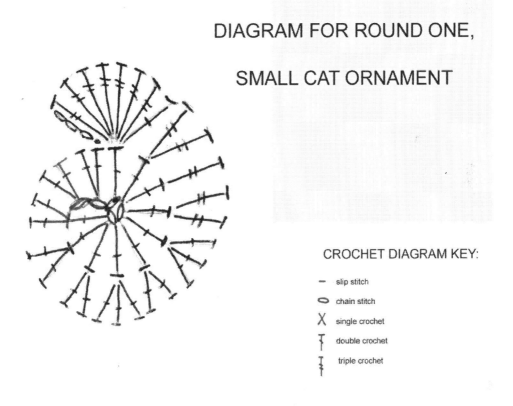

DIAGRAM FOR ROUND ONE,

SMALL CAT ORNAMENT

CROCHET DIAGRAM KEY:

—   slip stitch

◠   chain stitch

X   single crochet

†   double crochet

‡   triple crochet

threads which extend upwards from the center of the bird to the edge, where the rest of the stitch is looped and completed. These "long single crochet" stitches serve as decorative stitches which give the cat's back a sort of a stripey design, with chain stitch shapes visible only at the edges. It's fun! Try it! There's a link below to a video showing this stitch.

A helpful diagram is included above which shows the very few stitches which comprise the base shape of the cat worked in round one.

Materials:

To make a cat approx. 2" long, I recommend using **crochet thread** (one single strand or two held together) or fashion crochet thread (which is a bit puffier) and a **size 1 , 2, 3 or 4 steel crochet hook, depending on your preference and the size you wish for your ornament**. Smaller hooks are a good option for a nice tight teeny ornament; just experiment and find what feels best for you, but do bear in mind that changing thread gauge and hook size by very much can distort the design. But there are only a

handful of stitches in the whole cat, so try lots of different approaches!

Working your cat ornament:

Ch 3, join to form small ring.

Rnd 1: <u>Body:</u> Ch 2, 10 dc in ring

(Notice that you are approaching the original ch-2; you will not be joining, but will continue to work in a spiral to form a spiral shape!); *working at first in both loops of chains and stitches while working on spiral (see where pen is pointing in photo above).*

28

WORK 2 dc in 1st chain of rnd 1, 2 dc in 2nd chain of rnd 1, 2 dc in next 2 dc, (18 dc so far)

and from this point working in the back loop only,

work *(2 dc in next dc, 3 dc in next dc) repeat once from * for a total of 28 dc's,

then work 2 tc in dc, 1 tc in dc, 2 tc in dc. Then work (1 dc, 7 tc) **(if working in a particularly small crochet thread, you may need to make this 6 tc)** all in next stitch, then ch 3, join to same dc that all 7 tcs were worked in. (Head made). Turn so that you are working with the back side of the cat facing you, working counterclockwise across the top of the head just formed:

Rnd 2: sl st up side of last ch-3 just worked, and in the next tc, ch 4 (ear) sl st in both loops of next 3 tc, ch 4 for next ear, sl st in next st (both loops). You should be at the base of the head, where it meets the body. Slip st 11 times along back working toward tail. *An alternate is to lsc for the 11 stitches along back instead of sl st. (This will make long decorative stitches covering the dc's and tc's of the back .Notice that when you make long single crochets along the back instead of slip stitches, you will want to work 2 sc in the same place, then move to the next stitch – see photo)Also see a video explaining how to work these long single crochets:*

http://picasaweb.google.com/susanlinnstudio/VideoLongSingleCrochet?authkey=Gv

1sRgCPqYgJOW29GavQE# (this is a live link for e-book users only).

Continuing along the cat's spine, start sc's **in back loops** of edge of back (if you were looking at the front of the cat it would be the front loops -see photo at left) to form a dimensional tail. When you reach the part of the cat where the work spirals in toward the center - after

13 sc's - continue to sc for 3 stitches across the top of the work (see photo below), inserting your hook in the front loops of the

chains which define the edge of the spiral. Ch 1, join to same st, tie off.

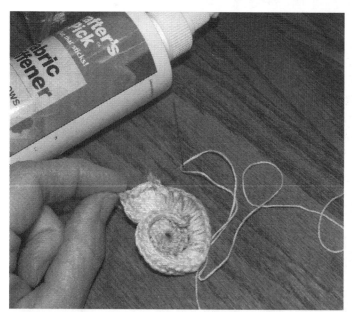

You will need to use fabric stiffener to give a point to the two ears, and possibly a little diluted stiffener to "puff" out the shape of the head.

Finally, a handful of embroidery stitches complete the eyes and help the nose of the cat: Using a needle and a bit of embroidery floss of your color choice, or even a strand of crochet cotton, make a stitch or two in the back of the cat's head to close or tighten the stitch in which all of the tc's were made for the head. Then move to the front of your cat and make a long simple stitch to indicate each closed eye. Tie off and weave the ends of threads through your work to hide them. If you wish, add a hanger of crochet thread. Enjoy!

Tiny Penguins

Pattern "P"

These tiny penguins are great when done in yarn or baby yarn. Since they only consist of a round or two, they work up to be tiny little darlings, approximately 2" long when made with **lightweight baby yarn**. I used a baby sport yarn in white, a **size 4 steel thread crochet hook**, and a heavy **fashion crochet thread** for the black parts. You'll also need an embroidery needle and some floss or crochet thread in black and gold for the eye, beak, and foot stitches.

Instructions for penguins:

<u>With color # 1 (normally this would be white):</u>

Ch 3, join to form a small ring.

Rnd 1: Ch 3, dc 11 times in ring, join.

Rnd 2: Ch 2, (dc, tc, dc) in next dc, ch 2, join to next dc and tie off.

Attach color #2 (normally black) to any topmost tc of the penguin body. Pull loop through stitch and tie knot at its base to form ornament hanger, if desired.

Rnd 3: sc in tc, sc in dc, sc twice in ch-2 from prev rnd. *(In this instance, make your sc's in only the outmost loops of those chains on the ch-2 so that your outline of black is not too bold)* Ch 7 (foundation for first wing), turn, skip 1 ch, sc in next 3 ch's, dc in next 2 ch's, sc in next ch, 2 sc in last chain, join to next dc of body. (wing made), continue for 3 sc in dc's, then (sc, 2 dc), in next dc, ch, sc in next dc, ch, (2 dc, sc) in next dc, sc in next 2 dc, ch 4. Turn, skip first ch just made, sc in next 3 ch, 2 sc in last sc on body of penguin (the one you made just before making chains for wing), (second wing made) sc in next dc, sc twice in ch-2 on other side of head (from rnd 2), sc in dc on head, join.

Finishing:

Weave loose ends through the back of your work to hide them.

Embroidery for beak, eyes, and feet (if desired):

With embroidery floss, tie a knot and insert needle from reverse side of penguin. Make one large stitch as shown for each eye (in black crochet thread or floss) and one large stitch in gold or orange for the beak, as shown in the photo. If desired, you can also place one or two straight stitches at the feet in gold or orange to give some detail there.

You may wish to cover the back of your penguin with felt. Simply trace the shape of your penguin in marker or chalk, and then cut it 1/8" smaller than the actual penguin. Stitch it carefully with dark thread, or glue it on to the back.

Easy Owl Ornament or Appliqué

This cute little owl appliqué or ornament is simple and easy (at least, the yarn version is), which is nice for a change! It is simply a disc of double crochets, with a second round of stitches on the edge. The thing that gives that puffy look to the belly and cheeks of the owl are distinctive long single crochet stitches similar to what you would do to form a crocheted button. (I explain this in a little video). Have a blast making these by the pile, and add a distinctive personality to each one with embroidered stitches that are a little different. Beads are the easiest way to add eyes to your owls, but you could embroider these, too.

Instructions for Owl worked in yarn:

This works best with a Medium weight yarn and a size F hook.

Ch 3, join to form a small ring.

Rnd 1: ch 3, dc 12 times in ring, join.

Rnd 2: Lsc (e-book users, see this video on making long single crochet stitches: http://picasaweb.google.com/susanlinnstudio/VideoLongSingleCrochet?authkey=Gv1sRgCP qYgJOW29GavQE#5532050358873346482) 16 times completely around circle, join.

Rnd 3: (see diagram below, on following page): Ch 1, skip first st, (dc, 3 tc) in next st, (3 tc, dc) in next st, ch 1, sc in next st. **(base head shape made).**

 Sl st in next st, Sc in next 5 st, ch 2, sc in same st, sc in next 2 stitches, ch 2, sc in same st, 6 sc, sl st at neck.

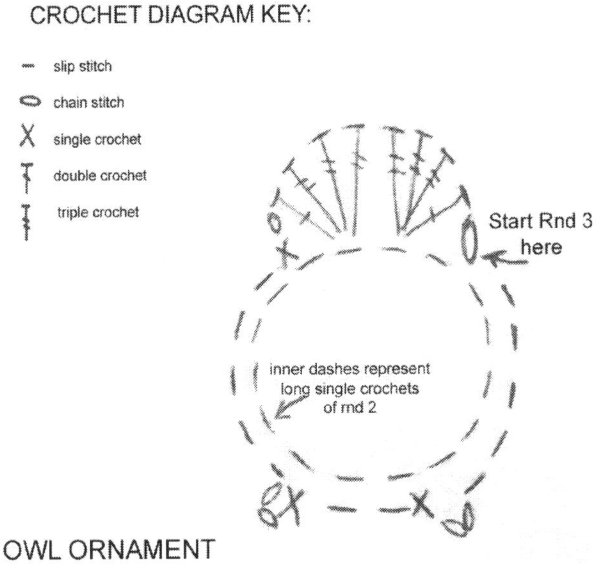

CROCHET DIAGRAM KEY:

— slip stitch

⬭ chain stitch

X single crochet

† double crochet

‡ triple crochet

Start Rnd 3
here

inner dashes represent
long single crochets
of rnd 2

OWL ORNAMENT
Round 3

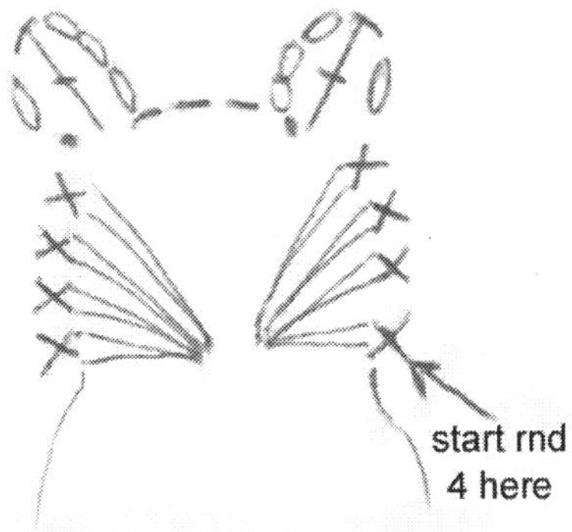

start rnd
4 here

OWL ORNAMENT
Rnd 4

Rnd 4: (see diagram above) Insert hook in the base of the (dc, 3tc) cluster on R side of head and make 3 long single crochet stitches (lsc's) in that place *(these will be long stitches which will go completely around the previous edge of the head -see photo at right- and give a decorative embroidered look.)* Slip stitch in top right corner of head, ch 1, dc in corner st of head (see diagram), ch 3, sl st in same st (at base of dc just made), **("ear" tuft made)**, sl st in next 3 st's across top of head, ch 3, dc in next st, ch 1, sl st in same place(**second tuft made**), lsc in next 3 st's (inserting hook in the base of the (3 tc dc) cluster on left side of head) . This will place you at the "neck" where you will tie off. Weave ends of your yarn through back of work. If desired, make a point on the "horns" of your owl by dampening the tufts and brushing on a bit of fabric stiffener, then pinching them to point them with your fingers. They'll need to dry for approximately an hour.

At this point a stitch or two of embroidery is also nice. As you can see in the photo, you may place two stitches in a V shape for a beak, and then sew on two beads for eyes. You can also place a couple of stitches to indicate the V-shaped "brow" of the owl above its eyes. Have fun and make your owl perky!

Instructions for Tiny Thread Crochet owl:

Use fashion crochet thread and a size 4 steel thread crochet hook to work a tiny owl approximately 1 ¼" inches long, perfect for a pendant, a keychain fob, or a tiny appliqué. These instructions only differ in that some sc's are replaced with slip stitches so as to give the miniature owl a more delicate shape.

Ch 3, join to form a small ring.

Rnd 1: ch 3, dc 11 times in ring, join.

Rnd 2: lsc 16 times completely around circle, join.

Rnd 3: Ch 1, skip first st from prev rnd, (dc, 3 tc) in next st, (3 tc, dc) in next st, ch 1, sc in next st. (**base head shape made**); sl st in next 5 stitches, ch 2, sc in same stitch, sl st in next 2 st's, sc in same st, ch 2, sl st in next 6 st.

Rnd 4: Insert hook in the base of the (dc, 3tc) cluster on R side of head and make 4 long single crochet stitches (lsc's) in that place *(these will be long stitches which will go completely around the previous edge of the head (see photo) and give a decorative embroidered look.)* You can find a link in the yarn owl instructions above to a video explaining this).

Ch 1, dc in corner st of head (see diagram), ch 3, sl st in same st at the base of dc just made (**"ear" tuft made)**, sl st in next 3 st's across top of head, ch 3, dc in next st, ch 1, sl st in same place(**second tuft made)**, lsc in next 4 st's (inserting hook in the base of the ((3 tc dc) cluster on left side of head to reach "neck" and tie off.

Weave ends of your yarn through back of work. If you wish, make a point on the "horns" of your owl by moistening the "ear" tufts and brushing on a bit of fabric stiffener, then pinching them to point them with your fingers. They'll need to dry for approximately an hour.

Also, as with the yarn owl, you'll want to add a stitch or two of embroidery. As you can see in the photo, you may place two stitches in a V shape for a beak, and then sew on two beads for eyes. The smaller of the owls in the main photo also shows how you can place a couple of stitches to indicate the V-shaped "brow" of the owl above its eyes. Read on for a thread crochet "Santa Hat" which works with the owl, the penguin, and the cat ornaments in this book!

Santa hat for Owl, Cat or Penguin Ornament:

This little hat is difficult! If you're not familiar with thread crochet and working small, you may want to practice a few times with yarn before attempting a tiny version of this little hat. For the hat, I use crochet cotton thread for the red part and baby weight (light weight) white yarn. In all parts, I used a steel thread crochet hook, size 4. In the owl and penguin hats you see above, the base of the red part of the hat was worked only in the back loops of the white base of the hat. In the cat, the base of the red part of the hat was worked in both loops, making a bumpier outline, as you can see.

For the Owl and Cat Ornaments, work the Santa Hat as follows:

Rnd 1: (Use white baby yarn - light weight - or white crochet thread) Attach thread to the back loop of sc just to the right of right-hand "ear". *Work the sc's in the back loops of these stitches.* Sc in same place, insert hook into threads in the back of the ear and sc twice in that spot, sc in next sc on the other side of ear, sc twice in center sc of head, sc in next sc, sc twice in place at center back of left ear, sc in stitch just to left of ear: **10 sc** along back of head and behind two ears. (see photo at left) Turn.

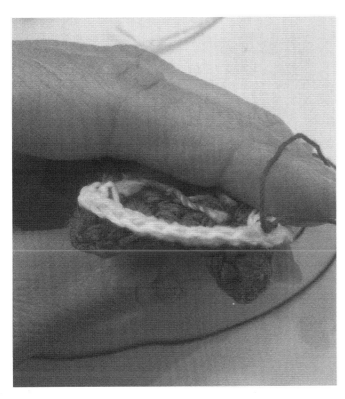

Rnd 2: ch 1, sc in both loops of every sc: 10 sc. Tie off and pull thread through to back side, weave end through work.

Rnd 3: (Use light weight red yarn or red crochet thread) Attach red thread to back loop of 2nd sc from the right on round just worked. Ch 1, sc in back loops of next 8 sc, turn.

Rnd 4: ch 1, skip 1st sc, sc in next 6 sc (working in both loops of sc's), turn.

Rnd 5: sl st in 6 sc just worked, sc along side of white hat band and to the base where it meets the head (3 sc) then continue to ch 6 for a thread crochet cat or owl, or ch 8 for yarn weight cat or owl, turn.

Rnd 6: skip first ch, sl st in next ch, sc back to base of hat (either 6 or 5 sc, depending on how many chains you just worked in prev rnd. Tie off at base of hat and weave ends through work.

Rnd 7: Attach white thread to very tip of red Santa Hat. Knot securely. Ch 2, and work 3-4 sc in 2nd ch from hook (depending on how large you want your white "pom pom" to be. Tie off and tighten work, and weave tail through base of "pom pom", knotting end securely to beginning end of thread. Cut off thread at approx. ¼", coat short ends with a tiny drop of white glue and tuck ends into pom pom. (an alternative is to weave the ends of the white thread through the work, which is hard!)

For the Penguin Ornament, the pattern varies slightly, since there are no ears:

Rnd 1: (Use white baby yarn - light weight - or white crochet thread). You will be working in the top center 5 stitches of the penguin's head. Attach thread to the back loop of sc which is two stitches to the right of center. Sc in same place, sc in next 4 stitches: 5 sc along top of head. Turn.

Rnd 2: ch 1, 2 sc in first sc, sc in next 3 sc, 2 sc in last sc: 7 sc. Tie off and pull thread through to back side, weave end through work.

Rnd 3: (Use light weight red yarn or red crochet thread) Attach red thread to back loop of 2nd sc from the right on round just worked. Ch 1, sc in back loops of next 5 sc, turn.

Rnd 4: ch 1, sc in next 4 sc, turn.

Rnd 5: sl st in 4 sc just worked, sc along side of white hat band and to the base where it meets the head (3 sc) then continue to ch 5, turn.

Rnd 6: skip first ch, sl st in next ch, sc back to base of hat (3 sc) Tie off at base of hat and weave ends through work.

Rnd 7: attach white thread to very tip of red Santa Hat. Knot securely. Ch 2, and work 3-4 sc in 2nd ch from hook (depending on how large you want your white "pom pom" to be. Tie off and tighten work, and weave tail through base of pom pom, knotting end securely to beginning end of thread. Cut off thread at approx. ¼", coat short ends with a tiny drop of white glue and tuck ends into pom pom. (an alternative is to weave the ends of the white thread through the work, which is difficult!

You may need to make adjustments to this pattern, as stitches become distorted and tightened as you work on the little animal ornaments, and the hat stitches may be altered to fit the reality of what your ornament's head is like. As long as the basic idea of two rounds of white sc, then two rounds of red sc and a round of slip stitch ending in the chain "tail" of the hat are followed, your hat will be fine! Be creative and enjoy your ornaments!

Thank you for purchasing my patterns! You can see more of my crochet designs at www.susanlinnstudio.etsy.com